BEEKEEPING FOR BEGINNERS

TABLE OF CONTENTS

INTRODUCTION

Bees can be regarded as fascinating works of nature which never cease to amaze scientists and bees' newbies with their industrious and sophisticated lifestyles. They are a disciplined set of flying insects with amazing ways of living; ranging from their communicating skills to their social organization. The bees are amazing but the fact that you can keep them and rear them into fruition is mind blowing.

Beekeeping is an exciting world on its own, it might seem daunting when it comes to mind, but learning about how it works can give you your own exciting life lasting hobby. Bees are easy to keep and friendly to pet, with the necessary equipment for keeping them, you will realize you don't have to break a bank before you can keep them. They don't require constant attention and monitoring and they do well in most, if not all climates.

Reading this book is a big step to unravelling the mystery that surrounds the exciting and fascinating world of beekeeping. Making profits with it is a big bonus attached to it. You get to have an exciting hobby and make money from it too, not to mention the nutritious food and the yummy products we get from the honey they produce. How mind shredding is that!

This book will take you into the world of beekeeping. You will have deeper insights about bees and their types as well as the advantages of beekeeping. Also, you will be enlightened about the challenges you are bound to encounter in beekeeping alongside the solutions and the tips for easy startups as a beginner. Not to forget the question that might be running through your mind; the legal consideration of beekeeping will be thoroughly and properly explored.

Other things that were discussed at length inside this guide include the life of the honey bees, how to get started with beekeeping, choosing a hive, bringing your honey bees home, bee inspection, honey production and much more! If you have ever given a thought or a glance at a beehive and wonder whatever goes on in there, or if you still have your doubts about keeping bees, or to not keep them, then this book is definitely what you need to tip your mind into adventurous, amazing and fun fact filled of the lives of the bees and how to keep them!

A BRIEF HISTORY

Humans have been involved with honey bees for thousands of years. In Spain, there are cave paintings of men that were harvesting honey from trees (dated to fifteen thousand years ago). Some Egyptian tombs pictograms show beekeeping management about 4,500 years ago. Up to the middle of the 19th century, beekeepers used containers made of clay to keep their bees. Bees were mostly obtained naturally by a swarm or by gathering a calm swarm of bushes. By the end of a season, honey and wax were taken from the bees by means of destroying most, if not all of the combs created by those little critters.

The ability of these wonderful creatures to withstand the harsh treatment meted to them by humans has been amazing and they have been able to acclimatize to the harsh environments of the world, existing in areas where humans live, from the equator to beyond the Arctic Circle. Most domesticated bees descended from a little number of queen bees from their first countries, which are Africa and Europe. Honey bees have survived via natural selection methods in those regions.

If these little creatures were to disappear from this planet, humans would have just four years until a severe shortage of food would start. Honey bees perform numerous pollination services; just think about the legumes, vegetables, seeds, nuts, and fruits we consume. Majority of these food items were pollinated by honey bees.

By the middle of the 19th century, some discoveries helped to drastically change the methods of keeping bees eternally. A simple discovery indicates that if there is a bee space of between 6mm to 9mm left, the little creatures won't seal it up with propolis (a gum-like substance) or even try to make use of the space by creating a comb across it. Thus, this finding resulted in the creation and designing of hives which allow the housing and movement of combs for inspection and this is the foundation of all recent hive design.

CHAPTER ONE: ABOUT THE HONEY BEES

Honey bees are popular but they represent only a little percentage of the bee species. They are the only surviving group from the Apini tribe, under the Apis genus. Honey bees are well known for secreting and storing honey and constructing remarkably huge nests with the wax produced by worker bees in a colony. Honey bees are members of the insect class, which is called Insecta. The insects are members of the subfamily Apinae, which create and store honey.

Honey bees are social critters that procure a caste structure for the accomplishment of tasks that guarantee the continued existence of the colony. Several thousands of bee workers which are all sterile females take charge of nursing, cleaning, feeding and defending the group. On the other hand, the male drones are responsible for mating the queen, who is the only fertile female in a colony.

What Does a Honey Bee Look Like?

A honey bee has a light brown color and measures about 15 mm long. It is an oval-shaped creature with a brown band and golden-yellow color. Though honey bees' body color differs between species and some of them have mainly black bodies, nearly all honey bees possess varying light-to-dark striations. The dark and light stripes help with the survival of the honey bees; the brightly colored body of a honey bee serves as a warning to honey robbers or predators of the honey bee's capacity to sting. This is unlike other bee species that hide upon sensing predators close by.

Anatomy of a Honey Bee

The body of a honey bee is divided into; 6 visible segments of the abdomen, 3 segments of thorax, antennae, legs, and stinger.

The honey bee's head consists of feeding structures, antennae and eyes. The eyes comprise the simple eye and the compound eye: the simple eye (ocelli) helps the bee to determine the amount of light present, while the compound eye enables the bee to recognize light, color and directional information from the UV rays of the sun. The bee's antenna helps to measure flight speed and to smell and sense odors. The bee's jaw, which is the mandible, is used to eat pollen, cut and shape wax, feed the queen and larvae, clean the hive as well as for grooming and fighting.

The bee's thorax includes legs, wings and the muscles that control movements. The forewing is typically larger than the hind wing and it is used as a cooling mechanism and also for flight, while the hindwing is used to cool the hive by fanning away heat. The six segments of the abdomen consist of a stinger in the workers and queen, female reproductive organs in the queen and male reproductive organs in the drone.

Behavior of the Honey Bee

The honey bee hives are generally found in rock crevices and in the holes of trees in the wild. The worker bees create hives from the wax secreted from their special abdominal glands. They also gather some flakes of wax produced from their abdomens and masticate the flakes until soft. These workers then shape the wax and use it to make cells to create the hive. Honey bees, unlike other species of bees, do not hibernate during the cold months. They only stay inside their nests, huddle closely together, share body heat and feed on stored foods.

Honey bees are social critters that live in colonies. Nonetheless, these little creatures display hostile behaviors in their colonies; a queen will sting other queens in the mating fights for supremacy, and the drones get ejected from their nests during the cold period. Honey bees play an important role in ecology and pollination, yet measures should be taken when handling them. Make sure you contact a pest control professional before you attempt to address a swarm.

Honey Bee Distribution

Honey bees species can be found worldwide and are seen in many places, including the United States and Europe. These species are most noticeable in late spring and summer when the new queens relocate from their old colonies to build new nests with thousands of worker bees. During this period, you will see large groups of bees swarming together to find a new nesting site and it takes a swarm of bees about 24 hours to discover a new nesting place. Although most swarms of bees are harmless, some species are exceptionally hostile and might attack unprovoked.

Since honey bees can be found all over the world, their behavior and nature may vary. For example, German and African honey bees are known to display remarkable defensive behavior while Italian honey bees are often more domesticated. Nevertheless, all honey bees can be extremely defensive when provoked and they are capable of chasing animals or humans hundreds of feet.

Pollination

Honey bees have been the major pollinators of flowers for millions of years and for that reason, the plants that produce the flowers have relied on the honey bees. Reproduction is the goal of the plant and the honey bees help to accomplish this goal by innocently transferring pollen (plant's male sperm cells) from one flower to another. Therefore, in the absence of pollination, most plants won't be able to reproduce and would die out eventually.

Human beings derive benefits from this relationship through honey production and crop harvest. Most of the crops we eat were pollinated by the bees. And this is the major reason many farmers maintain honey bee colonies because plants won't produce vegetables and fruits without pollination. Apart from pollination, honey bees take out nectar along with pollen from the flowers. They transport the nectar to their nests and convert it into honey through a process.

Honey Bee Dance

Two major theories are available on the way honey bee workers communicate with one another about a new source of food; the odor plume and the dance. Though there are proofs to support each assertion, the honey bee dance is generally more accepted. The honey bee dance language includes dancing and odor as a means of communication, yet the odor plume theory suggests that the bee enlistment solely depends on floral odor. The dance performs a significant role in the survival of the honey bee's species; it has remained one of the significant techniques used in food foraging.

Honey bees use the dance to communicate with one another especially when a new food source has been discovered. If a worker finds an abundant food source; when she returns to the nest, she'll dance in a circle to notify the others of her findings.

There are two types of honey bee dances; waggle dance and round dance. The waggle dance is when a bee waggles its abdomen like figure 8 pattern and this indicates that the food source is more than 150 meters. While the round dance is a movement in a circle which indicates that the food source distance is less than 50 meters from their nest. The accurate distance is communicated with the dance duration.

The dance language is understood by some humans. Researchers can verify the efficacy by measuring the quality and quantity of new nectar and pollen brought into the nest by the bee. Although, some characteristics of the dance language are still not known, especially the facts that these little creatures understand the entire dance patterns even in the dark.

CHAPTER TWO: RESPONSIBILITIES OF EACH BEE

Honey bees, like other bee species, are social creatures that live in colonies numbering in the thousands. There are three types of adult honey bees that reside in a colony; the queen, drones, and workers.

Queen Bee

The queen is the principal female bee and is considered as the mother of most or all of the bees in a colony. The worker bees choose an upcoming queen bee's larva and it's nourished with royal jelly, which is a protein-rich secretion. This enables the queen bee's larva to be sexually mature.

The newly hatched queen bee will start her life in a duel to the death with any other queens she can find in the colony as well as destroy potential rivals that are yet to be hatched. When she completes this task, she embarks on her virgin mating flight. A queen bee lays eggs and produces a pheromone that helps to keep all the females in the colony sterile throughout her life. Each colony has only one queen bee, which has the ability to lay two thousand eggs a day.

Drones

The drones are the male bees that are the products of unfertilized eggs. A drone has bigger eyes and does not have a stinger. These creatures do not have the parts of the body for the collection of nectar or pollen, so they can't help in feeding the community either can they defend the hive.

The only job of the drone is to mate with the queen. Mating happens in flight, which is why the drones have large eyes for better vision.

When a drone succeeds in mating, it dies soon because its penis and related abdominal tissues get ripped out of its body after mating. At the period of colder winters, the worker bees protect the food stores and stop the drones from entering the hive because they're no longer needed, making them starve to death.

Workers

The worker bees are females and they are responsible for doing all chores except reproduction, which is the sole responsibility of the queen bee. The worker bees tend to their queen in their first days and remain busy for the rest of their short lives.

The workers perform many roles which include guarding the hive against attackers like wasps, fanning the hive to maintain the right temperature, carrying water, foraging for food and nectar, removing the dead, storing pollen, building honeycomb, feeding drones, and preserving honey. Workers can also make the decision to move the colony in a swarm and then build a new nest.

To maintain a right temperature for the hive is essential for the continued existence of the eggs and larvae. The chamber for the young must be at a stable temperature for the incubation of the eggs. If the temperature gets too hot, the worker bees gather water and drop it around the hive, and then start fanning the air with their wings to bring about cooling by evaporation. On the other hand, if it gets too cold, the workers come together to generate body heat.

Other Important Information You Need to Know

The queen bee in a hive spends all or most of her time in the brood chamber. She is groomed and fed by young workers; in turn, she lays up to 3,000 eggs daily. Recent research has found that the presence of the queen bee in a colony is very important because she secretes an unidentified "queen substance" which helps to keep the colony in a healthy, productive state and prevent the workers from laying eggs. Some of the workers can lay eggs in the absence of a queen; however, such eggs can only produce drones (non-working males). This will make the colony become weak and dispirited. Without the queen's secretion, the bees get to know about this within minutes that they don't have a queen and this makes them loud, nasty and worked up. But you shouldn't worry about this since you'll be purchasing a healthy young queen with your colony and she'll live for about 2 to 5 years.

Since it is not advisable to keep the queen in the upper storage sections of a hive to lay her eggs, you may top the brood chamber with a device known as "queen excluder"; it's a flat frame that is the same length and width as the hive's other sections. It's covered with a heavy inset wire screen and the openings in the mesh enable the workers to pass through and drop excess honey in the upper stories but the opening is not big enough for the queen.

However, some experts have frowned at the use of queen excluder since it can result in swarming and possible loss of about half of the colony. Therefore, another option is to keep providing the queen with an empty comb in the brood chamber; this will make her stay and lay eggs there.

It is also important to note that honey should not be taken from the brood chamber where the queen is raising the young bees. You need to leave that part of the hive strictly alone while you check once or twice a week to check for signs of disease and to see how the laying is progressing. You can also divide the colony artificially before swarming time, though you can only harvest honey from a hive's supers.

CHAPTER THREE: ABOUT BEEKEEPING

Beekeeping dates back as far as 9000 years ago in North Africa with pottery vessels used as the means of keeping them. Beekeeping can be accompanied by a myriad of emotions; excitement, high hopes and anxiety. So, what is beekeeping? Beekeeping can also be regarded as the term apiculture. It is the maintenance of bees and their environments for commercial purposes. It can alongside serve as a hobby to keep one excited and well acquainted with the wonders of nature. It can also simply be put as the maintenance of bees and their environments to attain desired objectives, it could be for commercial purposes, relaxation purposes, and therapeutic purposes and also as a hobby.

The Benefits of Beekeeping

Beekeeping has a lot of benefits to humanity, it can't all be explained/ explored. In fact, beekeeping does the world a whole lot of good than it lets on. They are essential to humanity; remember what the great scientist, Albert Einstein said about the bees? If they all vanish, we all will have just four years to live. Their benefits to humans can only be left for the imagination. Some of the basic and known benefits are:

1. The Environmental Benefit of Bees: Bees help fertilize plants which helps in their growth and reproduction because they transfer pollen grains from one flower to another. It is estimated that most wild plants as many as 90% rely on pollinators like bees to grow and thrive, without bees, many of these fascinating wild species of plants will die off. Bees are also essential to agriculture and growing of food. Also, they don't have positive impacts on plants near them only, they can gather nectar and pollen grains from miles around, engulfing the ecosystem with sustainability.

2. Health/Therapeutic Benefit of Keeping Bees: Watching bees and how they work together with their environment can be like a soothing balm to the wounded soul because watching them gets one so engrossed and the present troubled state of mind can be forgotten easily. Their lifestyle, their intelligence and the fascinating way of honey produce has a calming effect on anxieties. Besides, when you keep bees, you are engrossed in them and their maintenance that you will find yourself momentarily forgetting about your troubles. And if you give your time and affection to them a lot, momentarily forgetting your problems will be an understatement.

3. Healthy and Aesthetical Benefits of Bees on Gardens: With the help of bees, attaining a full-scale garden is not so difficult to achieve. A beehive is enough for your growing flowers to flourish beautifully and grow healthy, talk less of having an apiary near your gardens; your flowers will never have the problems of pollination and even the presence of the bees flirting around your flowers will add more to the beauty of it all. The bees flying around the flowers and round the garden will give it a more aesthetic look and the feeling of being in a magazine -cover type of garden.

4. Medical Benefits of Bees: Bees have a lot of medical benefits attached to them. It is rumored that once a bee stings you, you have the tendency of remaining healthy for the rest of your life. This rumor cannot be too far from the truth because the medical benefits of bees covers most of the life cycle of humans; male and female with unique medical benefits to each and for both. The bee pollen gotten from the bees are said to:

a. Decrease the rate of menopause in women.

b. Increases sexual libido and enhances sexual enjoyment.

c. Used as a natural way of speed healing.

d. The honey gotten from bees boosts the liver's health and function.

e. Another medical benefit of bee pollen is the strengthening of the immune system.

f. High nutritional values are enjoyed from the bees in accordance to health values.

The medical values of the bees are wide, but the ones that scratched the surface has been listed above. Sadly, not everyone gets to enjoy these all round benefits of the bees and keeping them because they are allergic or deathly allergic to the bees and their produce.

The Challenges of Beekeeping

As a beginner and a newbie to beekeeping, you are bound to face some challenges in your beekeeping journey which is something normal; no one is born a beekeeping genius. What to do and what to not do about beekeeping are learnt, and the challenges you will face at beekeeping are also learnt. Advisably should be learnt before diving right into your beekeeping business/hobby. Not knowing these challenges beforehand can have devastating effects on the bees and their produce. And this might even affect your health, if you have chosen to keep bees as your hobby to keep your health issues in check. In fact, no one likes failures and to avoid a bad chain reaction during your beekeeping, this book will take you through the common challenges beekeepers face; especially the beginners and at the beginning of their beekeeping career.

As a new beekeeper, you are bound to encounter inadequacy in the knowledge and skills required for keeping bees. And sadly, most people after having little to no knowledge about keeping bees love to do the "do it your own" path, or "winging it". There is no such thing as doing it on your own, or winging it when it comes to beekeeping. While beekeeping might seem easy enough to you, there are some basic knowledge which you should acquire before deciding to start keeping your bees. And if the uncertainty of where to get the knowledge about beekeeping gnaws at you, especially if you are not the reading type, to save energy, time, money and to also prevent wastage, learn about beekeeping before you dive right into it. Learn from those who know it and are willing to share their knowledge about the keeping of bees with you.

You might also be faced with the challenge on where and how to get your first bee colonies. Not having the knowledge about it may let beekeeping seem daunting to you. The solution is to find the experienced ones to help you in these aspects as there are many ways to which one can get their bee colonies. They will know the in and out of it all, don't try to wing it out or work it out on your own. After being faced with this challenge as a beginner, it becomes easy from there.

There are many ways to which beehives can be placed, and you will face the challenge of how to place the ones that best suit you and your environment. The one which makes beekeeping easier for you alongside your other commitments; you have to learn and how to work it over. The perfect location which would not have a climate hazard or environmental hazards on your beekeeping activity will want to pose a challenge for you. You have to gloss over this fact and know the placement which is the best that goes and works for you. Also in this aspect of beekeeping challenge, find the location which will suit your beekeeping activity economically. The economic situation of a location might want to have a negative impact about keeping your bees. Find a friendly environment for your bees, and keep a friendly relationship with your neighbors. If you have placed your beehives in a non-bee friendly environment and an unhealthy relationship with the neighbors you have there, it might get you into trouble with the law. Don't get too confused about your beehive placement, you just have to know what suits and works for you and your bees.

The inadequacy of knowledge about bees and keeping them may pose a challenge for you when you don't know or can't recognize the queen bees in their colony. And the absence of the queen bee is a first class ticket to wastage and loss. When you have your new bee colony without its queen, there would be no increase in the colony, talk less of harvesting the produce you get from bees. With this is attached the commitment challenge. Not only the new beekeepers have this challenge at keeping and managing their bees. When a beekeeper lacks the spirit of commitment, he/she would suffer losses. And as for a new beekeeper who lacks commitment, when you don't notice the absence of the queen bee, it might be difficult for you to notice the decrease in them and by the time you do, it might have been too late. The commitment challenge is a big one, in relation to inadequate knowledge about bees and keeping them, connected to the absence of the queen bee in a colony.

Another challenge which might be daunting to a new beekeeper is winter, which is natural and has to happen. The reason why winter might pose as a challenge is because with winter equals nectar dearth. Nectar dearth is the shortage of nectar producing flowers. And a greater challenge that comes with this is the ability of a new beekeeper to recognize nectar dearth in summer. Nectar dearth in summer can be caused by natural disasters such as excessive heat and drought/low rainfall in the location where your beehives are placed.

Due to the cost of the activity in beekeeping is usually higher than the price of the produce gotten from the bees, it might be challenging to those in beekeeping for commercial purposes. The prices of honey and market is a challenge but once you are into it and have learnt the ropes of it all. This part of the beekeeping challenge might go down the drain.

Overall, the health and the maintenance of your bees and the beehives is very important and can be very challenging, especially with those with commitment issues. When you start keeping bees, you have to be mindful of their health and the keeping of the beehive is very important. The movement of some of the bees around the world might have exposed them to some chronic diseases, an example is "Varroa Mite". This disease is the number one enemy of the bees and their keepers. The spread is very dangerous and fast, if you are the type to neglect, again, this could be really challenging for you mind you, the Varroa Mite is just one of the many dangers to the health of your bees, so you have to be very careful and committed when it comes to their health and yours. No one wants failure, especially not in their first trial. Keeping your beehive healthy is challenging and essential.

All these might seem complex and the prospect of it all can get scary. But in the actual sense of it, they are not, once you have the downright experience of it, you are good to go. The all-rounder solutions to all is to go after the knowledge about keeping bees hotly. Find the successful and experienced ones about beekeeping to guide you through, read and watch videos about them. Also there are beekeeping associations you can join which will make the experience better and fun. If you wish, you can enroll in beekeeping classes. This will open the floor for meeting other lovers of bees and finding someone who you can share your fears and experiences about bees with doesn't sound bad at all.

Is Beekeeping Legal?

Now, let's go into the legal considerations of beekeeping. Keeping bees is legal, but that does not mean you can't get into trouble for it. Bees naturally are looked at with dread everywhere they go, of course, no one wants to get stung. Being careful is the only possible solution for keeping bees especially if you are a novice at beekeeping. And since most new beekeepers start by having their first small colony in their yard, it is advised to be extremely careful in the neighborhood and with your neighbors. Also keep a friendly atmosphere in and with your neighbors. They will less likely get you into trouble with the law when you do these.

Around the world, beekeeping is allowed and legal in most countries and cities since they contribute to the environment and the economy. But there will be rules and regulations concerning the keeping of bees as each country or state deem fit. In the U.S, beekeeping is legal, but your city will have ordinances which must be respected and followed by a prospective beekeeper of which an example is the restriction on the amount of beehives you can keep. Africa has the oldest colonies of bees in the world, beekeeping is legal in most, if not all African countries but each country and cities have legal considerations concerning the rules of beekeeping.

The answer is yes, beekeeping is legal, but there can be different approaches to them in each place. Beekeepers may be asked to sign compliance agreements, and there may be restrictions on the amounts of beehives one can keep. The best legal advice for a newbie in beekeeping is to be very careful in the keeping of their bees. Maintaining a low profile is also strongly advised when it comes to keeping bees.

CHAPTER FOUR: ABOUT BEEHIVES

The beehive is the home of the bees. So, when you are about to get started with beekeeping, ensure to create an environment that exceeds or at least meet the needs the bees seek out in nature. Choosing the right beehive saves you from issues while allowing you to concentrate more on the bees you're keeping. Below are the basic beehive requirements for raising healthy and productive bee colony:

- ❖ Shelter and safety

- ❖ Enough space for expansion

- ❖ Dry and well-ventilated conditions

- ❖ A nearby source of water

An Introduction to Beehives

Beehives are vital in keeping bees. Hives normally have a dome or boxlike shape. In the forest, bees build their hive by themselves anywhere they are pleased with. A bee may have its hive built in a hollow tree trunk or any place that serves as a shelter. As a beekeeper, you need to make provisions of a human-made hive for your bees to help you preserve the colony.

When you are about to get started with beekeeping, you should consider the type of hive you wish to use. This has different factors attached to it. You may decide to make your selections based on the hive type, weight, cost, etc. Common types of beehives include Langstroth hive, top bar hive, and Warré hive.

The Langstroth hive:

In the middle 19th century, Reverend Lorenzo Langstroth invented the Langstroth beehive in 1852. Langstroth hive is the most popular type of beehive currently being used by beekeepers. It has removable frames on which the bees build their honeycomb on. Langstroth hives are comprised of boxes that are orderly piled above each other. It enables the beekeeper to manage the bees in such new ways that were impossible at that time. Frames for Langstroth hives are crafted to stop the bees from placing their combs where they would have connected frames to the hive's walls or connect adjacent frames.

From its top to the bottom, Langstroth's hive has several parts: frames, foundation, outer/telescoping cover, inner cover, shallow honey supers, bottom board, brood chamber, and so on. Earlier Langstroth hives feature a portico entrance, integrated floor, and non-removable brood box, hinged roof, as well as a removable honey box. The honey box measures equal frame size with the brood box.

Furthermore, contemporary Langstroth hives are produced in various dimensions, which was different from the one initially designed by Langstroth.

Top bar hives:

Globally, top bar hives are the oldest hive design. It's lightweight. Using top bar beehive subjects the honey bees to build their honeycomb down right from the top bars. A horizontal top bar hive that has wooden bars, which are placed in line with the top of the long box. Top bar hives make use of one-piece bars. Building this beehive does not need any foundation. It only requires the hive to be raised above the ground by constructing a stand for it.

Additionally, the top bar hive offers many benefits to the beekeeper. Among them is that it exempts the need for foundation sheets and gathering wooden frames. Moreover, the beekeeper can conveniently carry it whenever they wish to change its location. Top bar hives also have limitations to some factors. Frequently, the beekeeper needs to monitor the hive to avoid overcrowding of the bees. It's more ideal in keeping bees for pollination purposes. However, it's also used to keep honey bees.

The Warré hive:

Also referred to as the people's hive. The Warré hive was invented in the middle 20th century by a French priest and beekeeper known as Émile Warré. It's a hive that has a top bar design. It possesses a vertical top bar rather than being a long horizontal top bar hive. The Warré hive is the outcome of his thirty years of experience in beekeeping practice. It was designed to provide an economical means of building hives through the use of regular tools.

Besides, they are not too expensive to build. Its design requires few accessories and low maintenance measures. It doesn't necessitate the beekeeper to check the colony regularly. With a Warré hive, beekeepers don't have to buy a costly honey extractor or apply a chemical-laden foundation. Warré hives demand nadiring, which involves the addition of more boxes to the bottom of the stack. It allows honeycomb to be consistently harvested. It also avoids reusing the old comb as they can be filled with toxins and chemicals from the environment and agricultural factors.

Setting Up Your Hive

1. The first thing to do in this step is to buy a hive. You may acquire a "starter kit" that will include all the components of the hive that is required for starting a beekeeping project. This kit can be gotten from some farm supply stores and also online. It consists of the essential equipment needed to get going with beekeeping. Although the exact components of the kit vary, it should have:

❖ Hive Boxes (2 or 3)

❖ Bee feeder

❖ Hive stand

❖ Hive Inner Cover

❖ Hive Outer Cover

❖ Bottom Board

❖ Frames

2. Purchase the tools you'll need to take care of your bees. After setting up a hive and placing the bees in it, there are some tools you'll need to handle them. These tools include;

❖ A smoker with a shield to make the bees docile whenever you want to go into the hive

❖ A mini crowbar which is used to take the hive apart

❖ A bee brush for moving bees around when you're dealing with the frames. The bee brush will enable you to remove the bees from the frames without hurting them.

❖ An extractor which is especially useful for harvesting a lot of honey. An extractor is a machine that you can place the honeycomb frames in it and it extracts honey from the comb with centrifugal force

3. Buy protective clothing. A beekeeping project requires purchasing the right clothing to protect you from getting stung by bees. As you get used to handling the bees you may not need all the protection anymore but it is important to start out with protection to ensure that you're safe around these little creatures. Some of the protective clothing you may need to acquire includes:

1. Bee suit

2. Gloves

3. Hard hat made to be used with a veil

4. Round tie-down veil

4. Choose a good location for your hive. A hive should be set up in a place with little human traffic and with nearby flowers. Make sure you pick a location that's relatively protected from high winds. If you have a garden, place your hive nearby but ensure it is placed behind a small fence or barrier to prevent the bees from

flying directly over your garden paths. The small fence or barrier will force the bees to fly up and over your garden path on their way to the garden beds. Keep in mind that the type of flowers that is near your hive will affect the flavor of the honey that your bees will produce. Generally, hives can be positioned in backyards, even with close by neighbors without problems. Your neighbors may not even notice them, but it is advisable to inform your neighbors prior to setting up the hive to ensure none of them are allergic to bees. It is possible for local, country and/or state laws concerning bees to exist in your district, so check with your community, state/region, and country for laws relating to beekeeping before you start your beekeeping project.

5. Start putting your hive together by placing concrete blocks or another strong base for the hive to sit on. The hive should be sited off the ground to prevent the wood of the hive from getting rotten and to prevent another insert from entering the hive. Also, put the bottom board on the base and then, place one of the boxes on the bottom board. Lastly, put the frames in the box.

Make sure you set up the concrete blocks so they're not completely level. When you have them slightly off of the level, it will enable water to roll off the hive top. Try to read and follow the directions that came with the starter kit. The bottom board should stick out farther to create an opening for the bees to enter and exit their hive.

Placing Your Hives in the Optimal Location

1. Make sure you expose the hive to the morning sun. Place the hive in a spot that receives morning sun. This will enable the little creatures to leave the hive early in the morning to forage for pollen and nectar. Therefore, position your hive in an area that gets full sun especially if you reside in a place with cooler climates like the north-eastern United States. But if you live in an area with warmer climates, place your hive in a spot that has afternoon shade.

2. Shield the hive from direct wind. Make sure you keep the hive away from open areas that are exposed to

breezes or direct wind. You can place your hive next to windbreaks like fences, bushes, trees, or shrubbery. This will help to guarantee the health and vitality of the bees and reduce the risk of the hive falling over. Let the entrances of the hive face south or southeast if you are living in Canada or the northern United States to shield it from winter winds.

3. Try spacing out the hives about one body width apart. This is to enable you to walk between the hives without grazing yourself. When you space out the hives comfortably apart, you will be able to move freely while working and it will reduce the risk of bees perceiving your presence as a threat.

4. Don't allow the hive entrances to face foot traffic. Position the hive entrance in such a way that it is facing away from people and animals that are likely to walk past it. This will reduce the danger that the little critters will perceive people and animals that walk past the hive as a potential threat.

CHAPTER FIVE: GETTING STARTED WITH BEEKEEPING

Keeping bees is like engaging in any other form of livestock management, a bee colony requires good shelter to be sound, well fed and disease free. A good beekeeper needs to understand the sound of bees, their behaviors, and their daily needs.

Honey bees are wonderful creatures that produce the honey we use as well as performing many other useful tasks like pollinating crops, for human beings. When keeping bees, you are helping their colonies to thrive and you also gain from them by collecting honey in return.

Starting a beekeeping project is very easy and it can be a cool project for you to do in your backyard. All you need to do is get enlightened with bees, how to take care of them and the supplies required to keep them thriving and healthy. However, don't forget to check your local regulations and notify your neighbors before starting your beehive:

1. Local Regulations

The first thing you need to do is to contact your local council office to verify the regulations and restrictions about keeping bees in your area. Then, find out about any beekeeping organization that exists in your district and how to join such an organization. Being a member of a local beekeeping organization would help you with all forms of information you will need in your beekeeping journey.

2. Inform Your Neighbors

Bee stings can be fatal for some individuals. Therefore, it is essential to notify your neighbors about your intention to start a beehive to enable you resolve any issue that any of them may have with keeping bees close to them.

Learn About Beekeeping

Before you start a beekeeping project, it is essential that you get to know more about them. You can take a beekeeping course. There are many colleges and universities that offer beekeeping classes for community education programs. Check out the ones in your state or region. Moreover, some beekeeping organizations host introductory classes for people who will like to start beekeeping projects. Therefore, perform an online research on classes for beekeeping in your area. Similarly, most schools of agriculture offer such a course. Although such class may be expensive, you'll learn many things you need to know about keeping bees.

Furthermore, try to learn some things from a beekeeper. Someone who is already into beekeeping will be able to give you one or two tips about caring for bees. This is especially important if you're planning to become a professional beekeeper. Typically, an experienced beekeeper will be able to answer any question you ask and should give you some useful advice you need to start up your own colony. You may consider offering to help a beekeeper with beekeeping for free in exchange for beekeeping information and advice. Some hands-on beekeeping experience before starting your own can be very useful, including the fact that the beekeeper will most likely appreciate the free labor you provided.

In many cases, the best approach to begin keeping bees is to join a nearby beekeeping association that has a beginner's courses and possibly has a preparation apiary where one can get some experience and learn from local beekeepers prior to starting your own project. In most cases, the only expense you may expend is for joining such Association because they'll have bees and skilled beekeepers that will show and guide prospective beekeepers on managing a colony as well as bee equipment to loan for the training. It is, however, advisable to go through a season in the training apiary before you spend lots of money to set up your own. It is even possible that the association sells new or fairly used bee equipment that you can purchase to start your own craft.

Make sure to start out with just a few hives. You may decide to become a beekeeper with just a hive or many hives. The amount you decide to tend to largely depends on how dedicated you are and what you want to get out of your efforts. However, if you are just beginning a beekeeping project, it is advisable to start small to figure out how you'll take care of your bees before you invest a lot of efforts and time in many hives. For somebody who just wants to obtain some honey for his/her family and wants his/her garden to be pollinated, one or two hives may be enough to achieve this. But for someone who wants to get enough honey for sale, many more hives may be required to produce enough honey to sell. Generally, a well-established hive may generate about 11 kg (25 pounds) of honey.

Essential Equipment for Beekeeping

The equipment and supplies for beekeeping are important to the beekeeping process. You can't keep bees without them, which is near to impossible. In beekeeping, there are the essential and the optional equipment you use; some are a must have, while some are optional, depending on the beekeeper, the use for the optional tools and the types of bees and the beehives he is into. Let's go over the essential and basic equipment for beekeeping.

1. **The Bees:** The bees are the most essential to beekeeping, you might have the rest of the tools and the equipment, and if you don't have your bees ready then you are not ready to start keeping your bees. What do you intend to rear with the equipment you have purchased if you don't have the bees themselves ready and available? Again, bees are essential and most important to beekeeping and the type of bees you want to keep depends on your choice.

2. **The Hives**: These may vary because it all depends on the type of the hive you want to use to house your bees; the purpose of your beekeeping activity might depend on the hives you will use. The hives for keeping bees as a hobby will be totally different from the ones used for

beekeeping as a commercial purpose. You need to do your research and choose your preferences.

3. The frames: The frames are also a part of the essential equipment for beekeeping. They are rectangular in shape and they hang inside the beehive. They can be bought or can be built from the scratch, there is the plastic frame and the wooden ones. It depends on your choice of frames for your bees.

4. A Smoker: A smoker gives you an advantage of being stung less by the bees. If you are going to go into beekeeping, you might want to get a smoker before you get started because the smoke from a smoker calms the bees and reduces the sting rates.

5. The Hive Tool: The hive tool is a very pocket friendly necessity in keeping bees. Its purpose is to pry apart the frames when the propolis made by the bees glue the frames and the hive bodies together.

6. The Protective Gear: This consists of the accessories adorned with the body for the protection from the bees and some possible diseases. This consists of the:

- ❖ The bee suit: The bee suit as the name implies is a special form of suit which covers the body and offers it a protective layer

- ❖ The Veil: This serves as the protector to the head, the neck, and the face from bee stings

- ❖ The Gloves: This protects the hands and the arms from stings and a studier one is advised during the course of your purchase because they will protect you better than the flimsy gloves would; they bear the brunt of the stings.

- ❖ The Shoes: Having a pair of shoes with extremely sturdy soles is part of the protective gear against the bees. You can't wear flip flops or sneakers to your apiary. Not wearing the appropriate footwear leaves your feet vulnerable to bee stings.

7. The Feeder: Nectars are not available throughout the time of the year for your bees to feed from and you will have to resort to feeding them yourself with the feeders. All you need to do is mix an equal amount of water and sugar to make syrup for them. There are different types of feeders, you can choose one that suits your convenience and that of the bees.

These are the basic and essential equipment you need to start your beekeeping activity. As you advance, you may have the need for more tools which you feel will be of much use to you. Also, as you progress and advance you might feel the need to upgrade your equipment to make things faster and easier for you and your bees.

Choosing the Right Honey Bees for You

As a new beekeeper, the confusion of getting the right honeybees might be overwhelming. Of course, who doesn't want to rear the best of the honey bees out there?

But there are different species of honey bees with different traits and each has its own uniqueness and methods when it comes to keeping them. You should take note there is a difference between "types of honeybees in a hive" which consists of: The Queen, The drone, and The Worker, and the different types of bees there is which talks of the species and the subspecies. A honey bee is a part of the species of bees which are about twenty thousand. Among these twenty thousand species of honey bees, only seven species of the honey bees are the most and widely recognized; this doesn't mean there are no other species of honey bees, but seven are the most popular of them all and they are:

- ❖ Apis nigrocincta - The Philippine honey bee

- ❖ Apis koschevnikovi - The koschevnikov honey bee

- ❖ Apis Mellifera - The western honey bee

- ❖ Apis cerana - The eastern honey bee

- ❖ Apis dorsata - The giant honey bee

❖ Apis florea - The red dwarf honey bee

❖ Apis andreniformis - The black dwarf honey bee

However in choosing your bees, there are certain conditions and cautions you might want to take. You have to consider your climate to that of the species you would love to keep. Some bees don't do well in the cold climate while some can thrive well in it. There are some types which are usually chosen by beekeepers; old and new, each with the preference and the condition that comes with the bees. Let's get familiar with some of these bees.

1. **The Africanized honey bees**: the Africanized honey bee is a hybrid of the Western honey bee; (Apis Mellifera). The African honey bees are usually defensive and they swarm the forest the most. They have a genetic dominance and they have by some beekeepers been asserted as superior honey producers and pollinators. They don't do well with harsh winters and extremely dry summers. They are known for their

protection and fierce possessiveness of their hives and they guide them aggressively too.

2. The Italian honey bees (Apis mellifera ligustica): This is a subspecies of the western honey bees. The Italian honey bees by far have the most points in the term of the gentility and cleanliness. They show a lower tendency of swarming unlike other western honey bees. Due to their gentility, they are most recommended and the most used by new beekeepers for startups which after some experience and favorable climate may move to the aggressive ones like the Africanized honey bees. The Italian honey bees in spite of their advantages too have their areas of weaknesses. For one, they lack vitality and are susceptible to diseases. Also, they don't do well in the winter and the nectar dearth might prove too dangerous to them.

3. The Carnolian honey bees: The carnolian honey bee is also a subspecies of the western honey bee. These bees drift less from one neighboring hives to another and are considered gentle and non-aggressive. However, they don't deal well with hot summers and the difficulty to recognize the queen might pose a challenge to a new beekeeper unless they are marked.

4. **The Caucasian honey bees (Apis mellifera caucasia)**: The uniqueness of a caucasian honey bee being able to extract nectar from the deepest of nectar tissues, where no other species can. This is an added advantage for the beekeeper and also, they are a very great user of propolis. However, the excess use of propolis makes it difficult for a beekeeper to clean and maintain their hive easily. The propolis glues the frames and the hives occasionally.

5. **Russian honey bee**: The Russian honey bees are more resilient to parasitical effects than other bees and can manage well during the short supply of nectar, therefore, they can survive and do well when winter comes knocking.

6. **The Buckfast bee:** The Buckfast bees descended from a line of bees developed by Brother Adam. They are a combination of several different races and strains of

bees. Brother Adam was a monk at Buckfast Abby in England. The Buckfast bees are much more on the docility side when it comes to their temper, and they have earned the reputation for their unusual homey-gathering abilities.

Each honey bee comes with its own characteristics, adaptation to climates and their own advantages and disadvantages. The one suitable for keeping depends on their adaptation limits to weathers conditions, honey production and of course their gentility. Also, the choosing of bees comes with the preference of the prospective beekeeper.

Buying Your Bees

For a new beekeeper, buying the bees for your apiary is the easiest and fastest way, not to mention a time saving way to start your beekeeping. Also, catching a swarm is a way of getting your bees which is a freebie but with it comes the great risks of their health, genetic or their temperamental problem. Being unaware of all these isn't great for a new beekeeper. There are ways in which you can buy your bees and save yourself the stress and the risks.

Source your bees early in the year; around January or February. It is best to buy bees in the spring when there is plenty of food around the new colony. Ordering packaged bees is the most common way of buying bees. If the company offers the marking of queen bees, jump on the offer because most new beekeepers don't or can't recognize the queen bees and neither will they notice the absence of the queen bee if such a situation comes up.

Another option when it comes to buying bees is the nucleus colony or "nucs" as it is being popularly called. The nucleus colony is more expensive than the packaged bees because with it comes an actively laying queen and a four to five frames of brood. So, the added cost is worth the offers that come with the nucleus colony.

Another option is the purchase of an established hive. With an established hive comes the actively laying queen, the bees, the frames and the hives. This is not strongly advised for someone with little to no experience on beekeeping. The age of the queen bee if not known can be risky because her death equals death of other bees. Also, they are usually more aggressive in the defense of their hives than the upcoming ones and maintaining a large number of hives can be challenging for a new beekeeper.

Create a Honey Bee Garden

This is created with the purpose of assisting the bees by creating a habitat for them to make their conversations and reproductions easier. You have to be careful in the selection of the flowers, the trees, the shrubs and the type of plants that you grow or select for the provision of nectars and pollen to your bees. A bee garden must have the flowers your bees will be attracted to, a water source or the provision of water and shelters which usually come in forms of deadwoods and logs. The preference of shelters in bees differs and the type of the shelter you will build for your bees depends on the preferences of your bees. Also, in the consideration of creating your honey bee garden, you should take note of the types of plants your bees will be attracted to; the color, the shape, the time of blossom and the species of plants. Don't have the wrong specie of plant for the wrong specie of bees. The risk of loss is high.

CHAPTER SIX: BRINGING THE BEES HOME

Make preparations

You are ready to bring home your bees into their home. Is everything prepared for their arrival? By now, you should have their hives ready, your protective gears ready and their environment cleaned and maintained for them. you need to put everything in place for their arrival, it will be unwise to bring them home before having to prepare all you need to have in place for their arrival. They might be on the top list for the essential equipment for beekeeping, of course there is no beekeeping without the bees, but that doesn't allow the place for sacking. Everything should be prepared for the arrival of the bees, not only their environment and their home, you as a new beekeeper should be prepared mentally for the arrival of your bees because that starts the real journey of the beekeeping.

Transporting Your Honey Bees Safely

Most apiaries ship with the U.S. Postal Service while some ship with a private carrier. So, you may have to go to the post office to get your package since many mail carriers do not like to deliver live bees. It is safer to transport your bees using a car especially for long distance journeys and the transportation will seem tasking and daunting to new beekeepers if proper preparations are not made, especially being their first.

1. Close all holes in the hives after proper investigation to prevent the escape of the bees during transportation. Staple mesh or tulle fabric for the covering of the holes is recommended for proper airflow. Using a tape can be dangerous to the airflow of the bees while transporting.

2. A smoker will be used in calming the bees before/during the transportation. A little bit of smoke

can be aired to them before the hive is sealed for transportation.

3. Bees are highly intelligent animals which always find a way in most situations where they find themselves. A duct tape of high quality is recommended for the sealing of the seams of the hive which won't allow escape for the bees while transporting them. Ensure there is no space or gap for them to squeeze through. Also. Being patient for warm weather before the transport of the bees is advised; the bees are more dormant during the cold times.

4. When you are driving your bees to their new home, drive slower and maintain a cool temperature in your car. It is also better to drive your bees home alone because due to their sensitive and intelligent nature, bees can sense aggressive energy from wherever it's drifting from. If you have someone in your car and the person gets overly uncomfortable making them aggressive, the bees can sense the aggression radiating

off them and they will get highly defensive and aggressive too.

5. Bees should not be kept in the car trunk because the trunk offers little to no proper ventilation. And for this reason, you are advised to transport your bees alone. Even though you spray them occasionally to keep them cool, do not make long pit stops on your journey. The hive isn't allowed to be placed under unnecessary duress.

Installing The Bees into The Hive

You are officially this step away from being named a beekeeper. It is common knowledge to know that the bees and the necessary equipment are all available, in place and ready for use. Now, let's go over the steps for installing your bees into the hive. Be in your protective gears; the veil, the bodysuit, the gloves and the shoes.

Syrup satisfied bees are prone to calmness and quiet; they feel at peace. So before you install your bees into the hive, spray them with syrup; sugar and water mixture. The bees will feed on this syrup and this will keep them calm, quiet and controlled.

Separate all the frames from the hive and spray each frame foundation with the syrup. Restore the frames after spraying them with water and sugar mixture. Mind you, the container or bottle you will use in spraying the bees and the frames is advised to be a new one; an old one which is washed is more open to chemicals which could leave a terrible reaction on the bees.

Use your hive tool to remove the wooden panel/cover from the first package, and remove the feeder and the queen cage from the hole provided in the box. Then, inspect the queen cage to see if the queen bee is still alive and healthy, next replace the wooden panel of the package to prevent the escape of other bees.

The bees need to be at the bottom of the box for easy installation, so before you install them into the hive, knock the bee package on the ground to make the bees drop to the bottom of the box. Make sure you are holding the wooden panel in place while doing this.

To finally install, after you have shaken the bees to make them settle down to the bottom of the package, turn the package upside down over the hive body. Shake the bees into the space of the hive and let them come out and settle on the sugar water stained hive body.

Congratulations on your first contact with the bees! You are now officially a beekeeper!

Feeding New Bees

As a new beekeeper, feeding your new honey bees is an important task and responsibility. It is fortunately a simple task, nothing special; sugar and water mix is what you feed them. You can also call it syrup. Feeding your new bees helps them adjust better to the kick off of the season and makes them a lot more energetic. The settlement of the bees into their new home doesn't stop the feeding of the syrup, every year, certain weather/climate conditions require the bees to feed on the syrup.

At the beginning of the beekeeping process, the bees are fed until they can draw out their own comb and also start filling it with nectar on pollen. It is more advisable to not leave the syrup in the open for them to feed on, this might attract other bees and cause the spread of diseases in the apiary, also a form of bee robbery. You should feed the bees often and keep a tab on how fast they finish their sugar-water mix and also to check the comb for the amount of syrup that has been stored.

Overfeeding your new bees is advised and should be taken seriously especially when there are no nectars around or available for them to feed on at that time. Being easy on the feeding may lead to starvation and cause a massive number of deaths among them.

Spring Feeding Your Bees

When you have gotten your colony settled in its new home around the middle of April, which is considered a lean period for honey bees in most places since there are little nectar and pollen to gather. For your colony to develop its strength rapidly, you need to continue feeding the bees artificially for the first few weeks of their arrival. This will help to fuel early laying of eggs.

The easiest method you can use to nourish the bees is to feed them with syrup using a bee feeder. The bee feeder is just a wooden insert for the entrance of the hive. This tool is punctured with a flow channel to convey sugar syrup to the hive's interior. When you turn the block upside down, you'll find a cap from a Mason jar that has been punctured to allow the contents to trickle out.

This container will be filled with warm syrup that you have prepared with equal part water and granulated sugar. Heat up the water and granulated sugar until all the crystals get dissolved. However, be careful not to scorch the syrup or it will hurt your bees. In case you're considering refined sugar not to be the best diet for your bees, just know that it really helps to get rid of starvation and is recommended by almost all professional beekeepers.

Pollen is a much better food you can provide your bees even if you are using sugar syrup. There are some beekeeping supply firms that sell pollen at an affordable price. The USDA also suggests the following supplement for spring feeding bees.

- ❖ Sugar/water: Dissolve 2 parts sugar in 1 part water by weight

- ❖ Pollen/soy: Combine 3 parts soybean flour with 1 part fresh dry pollen by weight

Pour the mixture through a cloth and drape it over the frames in the brood chamber. And this is indeed the best way to nourish your bees for the first few weeks in spring.

You may also try out the following pollen alternative. However, keep it in mind that it is less satisfactory than the one mentioned above, it is recommended sometimes.

- ❖ dried egg yolk: 10%

- ❖ dry skim milk: 20%

* brewer's yeast: 20%

* casein: 30%

* soybean flour: 20%

It is more advisable to use the formula that contains pollen if you can. This will enable the bees to get on their feet and start laying eggs as fast as possible to enable more worker bees to be ready for the spring honey flow. When you feed your bees pollen early in the season, expect good results.

NOTE: It is very important to be aware that your bees must not be fed with pollen in the fall. Anything other than sugar syrup or pure honey will kill them. Because these fussy little creatures do not excrete inside their hive, they can go for a whole winter without excreting any waste. Any adulterated food item will give the wintering bees diarrhea, and if the weather is too cold for them to go outside to release their waste, they will die in the hive. Another study suggests that pollen does not cause winter diarrhea but unripe honey, or that the colony may be too weak to withstand the cold leading to inability to constantly fan, which makes the bees eat too much.

The best food for the bees in the cold months is the same honey the workers stored earlier in the year. And a typical colony requires about 30 to 45 pounds of pure honey and a bit of sugar syrup to make it through the cold months successfully. Therefore, a deep super which is filled with about forty pounds should be enough but most beekeepers suggest two super as a safer option. And you can paint the other empty chambers if needed and keep away in preparation for the next honey flow in spring.

CHAPTER SEVEN: THE BEE INSPECTION

How Often Should You Inspect the Hive?

As a new beekeeper, you are excited to check out and inspect your bees and the activities time to time. While the periodic inspection of the hive is good, too much excitement in inspecting your hive is not a good thing. The inspection of the beehive to understand the functioning of the colony on a regular basis is good but overdoing it can be dangerous to the health of your bees. There is no particular formality for the inspection of bees, the type of hive determines the type of periodic inspection they get.

In contrast to your own excited mood, the bees can become very unhappy when you inspect too much. It will be best for you to learn the hive and the behavior that comes with each because inspecting disturbs and disrupts the bees' activities and that makes them sad; aggressive even. With time, the life of the bees and how they act will make much sense to you. Signs of aggressive behavior or abnormal odor, death among them and other strange things might occur if you don't inspect the hive routinely. Strike a balance between the two; plan out your inspection schedule and not overdoing it. Being far from the hive can be dangerous and being too close can be uncomfortable. Therefore, 7 to 10 days is recommended for hive inspection. Bees are a set of classy and picky creatures; they need attention, but not too much of it.

Preparation for a Hive Inspection

In getting ready for your hive inspection as a newbie to this aspect, there are some steps you should take when getting ready for a hive inspection:

❖ Get your protective gear ready. Being protected from the bee sting will protect you from having the trauma of being stung with bees every time. When you have the trauma of being stung by bees, you will have difficulties in going for the regular inspection of your bees which may result in catastrophe.

❖ It is necessary to have your tools ready. The basic ones are your hive tool, the smoker, lighter/matches, the mixture of the sugar and water if you were going to feed them at the moment, and also your notebook and your pen or pencil for your beekeeping journal.

❖ Be wary of the emotions you feel when around your bees. An overly excited mood or an apprehensive one will trigger the aggression in them, normally they are not happy about the disruption of their activities so when you add a swirl and gust of emotions to the mix, they may not take to that kindly. Which is why a smoker is an essential equipment in all aspects of beekeeping.

❖ Note that the bees see the red color as black which they are not attracted to. The black color does get them on the defensive side and they do so aggressively. When going for your beehive inspection, do not wear anything with the red or black color.

The Inspection Process

Begin your inspection by removing the frame closest to the outer wall; it doesn't matter which side. Gently put it down on the ground and work on prying or losing two other frames, it gives you better access to the hive. Put the frames up for inspection by holding each frame up with your back to the sun so that the sun can illuminate the frames for better scrutiny. You will see the small larvae, the cells 'details and the eggs.

In inspecting your bees, when you notice you are being watched by them, gauging your reaction, a little bit of smoke keeps them at bay. Understand what to look for in your hive; look for indications that the queen bee is alive and healthy. That is the whole point of keeping bees. Inspect their attitudes in case the bees are being abnormal, inspect their food and their environment.

About Smoking Bees

Smoking bees is an easy method of calming your bees when you want to check them. The smell of smoke from the smoker causes them to assume that the hive is in flames and they intuitively begin a fire drill. Rather than protecting their home, the little creatures begin to consume honey in preparation for swarming to find a new site. But once you are done with the inspection and stop the smoke, your bees will go back to their normal activity.

How to use a smoker

You can easily do this by puffing some smoke around the hive's entrance for about five to ten minutes before you open the hive. This procedure will start the fire drill and they'll possibly be filled with honey by the time you open the hive and they won't be able to sting you. When you open the hive, make sure you puff some smoke on the top of the frames as you inspect the hive.

Traditional smokers: This device is a metal container with attached bellows for lighting a small fire. This is to aid the fuel to burn well and produce plenty of thick good smolder. Different items like tightly packed dry grass, cardboard, dried leaves, or an old hessian sacking can be used to generate smoke. Make sure the smoke is cool and doesn't burn your bees. The act of mastering a traditional smoker is somehow the most difficult aspect of keeping bees and requires practicing to start and keep it alight.

Liquid smoke: In case you don't want to use a traditional smoker, you may try out the liquid smoke. This does not require any lighting, it isn't possible for you to get burnt and the smoke won't ever go out. All you need to do is to purchase the concentrated liquid smoke and dilute with water. This liquid smoke is created from condensed smoke produced by wood as it smolders. It's totally natural and can not cause any harm to the bees. To use it, just spray it with an ordinary garden sprayer. It is much simpler to use a liquid smoke compared to the traditional smoker even though it doesn't have the popularity that the latter has.

Start Your Beekeeping Journal

As a beekeeper, there are stages to your beekeeping journey. And during inspection, it is good to pen down what you have noticed and what you didn't, the progress of the bees, the pattern of their attitudes, their feeding capacity. All these should be kept in your bee journal to keep track of the hive and its activities.

Activities of the bees which may be unfamiliar to you at the beginners stage of your beekeeping. You should get familiar with their sounds, their smell, their mode of communicating, and their time of being docile and their time of being aggressive.

Also, there might be unforgettable memories and moments associated with your beekeeping journey which may be sad, challenging or happy and a time of breakthrough. Penning all these down in a bee journal helps to take note of the specific time and dates of the happenings. To take more preventive measures and to work towards more achievements on the hive.

About The Beekeeping Year

Honeybees being temperature depending creatures have varying monthly activities from year to year. The actions of the beekeeper will also vary due to the types of bees they keep as well as their beekeeping practices. This is why the beekeeping journal is highly recommended for the update and the upkeep of the inspection of the hive and the activity. It is good to take note of each month, the discovery and the challenges.

- January: Beekeepers should regularly check their hive this time for the availability of the winter stored food. If there is the scarcity of food in the hive, they should feed the bees with syrup. The honeybees at this time of the year rarely go out, they go out only when the weather is a little bit favorable; milder, for the passing out of excreta. A few may go in search of water and maybe some early pollen; hopefully.

- February: The availability of water should be made in sunny areas in the hive. The queen bee actively lays more eggs each day and the bees now fly more from the hive due to the warming up of the weather and the days getting longer. The bees seek more sources of pollen than the ones they are used to.

- March: The queen bee now lays more eggs but as the winter bees die off, the number in the colony might still be low. The bees will fly off more as the weather becomes more suitable and there is now improvement in the amount of pollen. If the food or store is still low, the beekeeper should feed his bees the syrup; sugar and water mix.

- April: There should be more availability of nectar due to the early blossoms of the year and the bees build up impressively fast and the drones start to surface.

With the favorable weather, the beekeeper should begin his weekly inspections as the colonies with rapid buildup may produce swarm cells. Also, the beekeeper will want to take note of the increase of the colony due to the actively laying queen.

- May: As a new beekeeper, this is the right time to start watching out for the varroa mite. The favorable weather of May paves way for the rapid increase in the stores and the bee numbers. Weekly checks should continue as this is mainly the swarming month and the beekeeper should be ready with the equipment for artificial swarming.

- June: In June, there is not much forage around and the beekeeper should watch for this period. This period is also known as the "June gap". If the varroa has invaded, quick action for the curbing should be taken by the beekeeper. The bees may still continue to feed if there is unavailability of stores. This may be due to the extracting done in May.

- July: The weather is more favorable in July and there is surplus supply of nectar for the bees. There will be reduction in the colonies as most bees would have no desire to swarm. The beekeeper is advised to go for his weekly checks because of the "what ifs" case that might arise. More bees now feel inclined to forage because the laying of eggs by the queens reduces and slows down.

- August: At this time of the month, the queen's egg laying gets lesser and lesser and the colony keeps getting smaller. The beekeeper if he wishes to can now take a break on the weekly inspection and take a breather on the activity. The treatment of the varroa can start towards the end of the month while there is still an increase of the temperature. The entrances of the hives can be reduced to help the bees fight off the wasps thieves.

- September: The beekeeper, if there is insufficiency of honey for the winter, will have to feed the bees with heavy syrup; the varroa treatment should continue. And there may still be issues with the wasps.

- October: There is the preparation for the winter and the bees are adding to their stored pollens and nectars till the end of this month. The beekeeper can still feed if he thinks the winter stores won't be sufficient.

- November: The bees will cluster round the queen bee; who by now might have stopped laying her eggs, on colder days. The beekeeper should do an inspection of the hive and make sure it is well ventilated. The hive should be weather secured and tight.

- December: The bees only go out on milder days only to pass out excreta but mostly are clustered around the queen who by the end of the month will start laying. A thorough cleaning of the hive equipment used during the year should take place and beekeepers should check fortnightly to know the security state of their hives. The notes taken throughout the year should be consulted and the preparation and planning of the coming year should come through.

Bee Swarming

As a bee colony grows stronger, it can outgrow its quarters to the extent that the queen bee and a large number of workers and drones will swarm (leaving to find a new nesting site). Swarming usually occurs at the start of honey flow and it happens as a result of insufficient space or too much heat inside the hive. When the bees are ready to swarm, they start to cluster in golden masses at the front of the hive. During this period some days of valuable foraging are lost and if they succeed in a swarming attempt, more than half of your colony will be lost. Therefore, a good beekeeper will try to hold down this impulse as best as he can. Below are some things you can do to prevent swarming:

1. A colony usually swarms as a result of too many bees trying to crowd in a hive with small size or with

inadequate space. When you add a new foundation or a few empty supers of used comb, it will make the restless bees to be satisfied to stay instead of splitting the colony.

2. Swarming can also be prevented by clipping the mother's wings or confining her inside the hive by using a queen trap, a perforated metal gadget or a wire that fits the entrance of the hive and that permits just the smaller worker bees to pass through. After you have taken these precautions, your babies may fly into the air cheerily, bustling like a low-flying plane; however, once they become aware that their queen is nowhere to be found, they will awkwardly find their way back home and forget the whole swarming thing till the following year.

3. If any swarm, however, succeeds in leaving the hive, they won't be able to go far initially. This is due to the fact that the mother is not used to the bright daylight and she finds it hard to fly for a long time; the only times she flies is during mating and swarming. Therefore, wherever the queen lands, the remaining bees will

surround her. She stays there buzzing on a bush, rock or tree branch, waiting for the scout bees to come back with news of a new nesting place. If you are able to find part of your bees in this state, simply get an empty super with foundation frames and carefully cut the branch they're clinging to. However, if their position will not allow you to gather them in a cluster, simply get a cup or ladle and spoon them tenderly into a cardboard box or basket. Don't worry; they will not sting you because a new swarm is satisfied and relaxed. This is true since the worker bees have prepared for the swarming by filling themselves with enough honey to create a new comb in their home and it's generally known that honey-gorged bees will not sting except when greatly annoyed. So, don't think you can handle them roughly because if you do, they will surely retaliate.

4. After you have secured your bees on the branch or in a box; shake some of them into a new hive, place the rest of them on a white sheet and lay it directly in front of the hive's entrance. If you're able to find the mother; once you hive her, the rest of them will follow suit. Make

sure you hold her carefully by the wings or thorax and avoid touching her abdomen so as not to injure her or ruin her ability to lay eggs. But if you can't find the queen, don't worry as bees typically take the clue and will enter the hive eventually.

5. If the newly hived bees stay where you place them for a few days that means you've doubled your colonies free of charge and very fast too. The remaining workers in the first colony will instantly nurture a new queen. However, the only disadvantage of having two separate smaller colonies is they will produce less honey compared to a single large colony. Even at this, many beekeepers believe that separating a colony in this manner is a cheap way of filling hives and they suggest doing this just before the bees will be ready to swarm.

CHAPTER EIGHT: ALL ABOUT HONEY

About Honey Production

Simply put, the honey is the sweet labor for the keeping of the bees. The honey is a sweet thick sticky liquid substance which is golden in color. The bees produce the honey by making use of the nectars of flowers which they save into their hives for eating during scarcity.

As a colony develops, the storage cells in the brood chamber get filled up in no time and you will need to add one frame at a time for you to remove surplus honey. This stage normally takes place between mid-June and mid-July in northern states and you can share out of your babies' harvest shortly afterward. If you so desire, you may take out a frame that's filled with honey; cut out the comb into hunks and sell or enjoy it like that. If you want to do this, ensure you make use of the thinnest foundation you can purchase so you don't feel like you're eating the spine of a fish.

Equipment for Honey Extraction

You should know the glossy and the attractive honey you are used to seeing don't appear magically immediately after their production by the bees; they are extracted and there are equipment for extracting honey. There are the basic equipment and the optional equipment. The optional equipment might depend on your need for them in extracting honey. The basic ones are:

- The protective gear: It is an established fact that your protective gears should all be in their appropriate positions when going near your bees. Going near them without protection is very risky. In keeping bees and in extracting honey, the protective gears can be said to be an important equipment for extracting bees.

- The honey extractor: A honey extractor is an important equipment in extracting honey; they use centrifugal force in squeezing out honey from the comb. Your honey extractor may depend on your preference or budget. They come in varying sizes and models.

- The honey uncapping knife: For slicing through the wax cappings efficiently, smoothly and cleanly. It might be electric, it might be manual.

- The honey strainer: This is used for straining the extracted honey to get out little bits of woods, wax and other things that might have gotten mixed with the honey.

- The bottling bucket: This is used for storing and bottling the extracted honey. They are buckets with airtight lids and are made from food grade plastic. Each can hold up to sixty pounds of honey and they are featured with a honey gate.

Harvesting Honey Step by Step

1. Open the hive: You should be clad in your protective gear; most importantly. Open your hive and be slow and deliberate in your movements, you don't want to aggravate the bees.

2. Remove the frames: Carefully and gently remove the frames from each hive and place them gently on a neat surface. But before you do this, it will be better to get the bees out of there so as to not risk injuring them, or them attacking you. Use a smoker to get them away from the processes of your extraction, a bees brush can also be used to brush them off gently so as not to injure them.

3. Uncap the honey: Use your honey uncapping knife to uncap off the honeycomb sealed with wax.

4. Extract the honey: Extract the honey by putting the frames into your extractor. The mode with which you go through this process depends on the style and the model of the extractor you use. When you have placed the

frames into the extractor, spin the frames and this will squeeze the honey onto the wall where they trickle down to the bottom of the extractor.

5. Filter the extracted honey: This is when the strain comes in handy. Filter the honey using the strain to separate particles from the freshly extracted honey.

6. Bottle your freshly extracted honey: make sure your bottling bottle is sterilized and clean for your honey to be free from the risk of being contaminated.

What You Can Do with Honey and Other Bee Products

The honey serves a whole lot of purpose. You can sell them and have a satisfactory monetary reward for your hard work. The honey also solves a lot of complex beauty problems; the honey when mixed with other ingredients solves moisturizing problems and keeps the face smooth. Also, the medical benefits of the honey are uncountable; the basic ones being the use of honey for sore throats, burns, rapid wound healing, inflammation, and facial care; for those with the serious issue with acne and zits. Honey also serves as delicious treats, either being licked straight up or making delicacies and delightful snacks out of them. Categorically, the benefits of the honey can be listed into:

- ❖ The monetary reward.

- ❖ The medical benefit

- ❖ The health benefit

- ❖ The cuisine benefit

Apart from the honey, there are also a lot of other bee products which all can't be mentioned or known, with their uses attached to them. The popular of them are:

i. **The beeswax.** The beeswax, just like the honey, is rich in the qualities and the quantities in their uses. Some of them are: candles (aesthetic use), for hair growth and for skin maintenance (beauty purpose), for pain relief, diarrhea, eases swelling and calms hiccups (medicinal and health benefits). The yellow beeswax can also be used as a stiffening agent in food when treated with alcohol.

ii. **The bee venom.** The bee venom is an agent in desensitizing bee stings.

iii. **The royal jelly**. The royal jelly serves as an amazing dietary and nutritional ingredient, especially for the elderly.

iv. Also, **the propolis** created by the bees is a natural antibiotic.

CHAPTER NINE – KEEPING YOUR BEES HEALTHY AND SAFE

As a beekeeper, keeping your bees safe, healthy and buzzing should be your number one priority. That is the main purpose of keeping and rearing them into fruition, be it physically or emotionally and that can't be achieved if they all fall sick and die. That will be a great loss to your pockets, your time and your energy. Also, it could be a loss for the mental health too; on the part of those keeping bees for health purposes.

Why Do Bees Get Sick?

Bees, even though they are strong, also do get sick. And there are many reasons as to why the bees might get sick, some being:

❖ Starvation: When there is unavailability of the nectar or the honey in store due to unfavorable weather, they will starve if the beekeeper relents in his responsibility as their keeper and doesn't feed them syrup due to neglect or lack of commitment. And when they starve, they get sick and if not monitored or noticed on time, leads to death.

❖ Too much excitement on the part of a new beekeeper: It was said in Chapter Seven that bees get sad when their daily activities or routine is disrupted by the beekeeper and may get sick of it when it becomes too much. If you are excited about being a beekeeper, lessen your excitement when it comes to the inspection of your bees. When they get sad over and over again, the negativity of the emotion might weigh them and from there they become sick. Keep yourself in check about inspecting your bees even especially when there is absolute no need to do so. You don't want to get your bees sick.

❖ Also, their polluted or contaminated environment or home might get them sick. More so, if there are wrong species of trees and flowers planted in their garden, this will get them sick and may lead to death.

Signs of Sickness

The bee will become sluggish other than their usual buzzing way of life. There are differences in bees being docile with smoke or being calm after being fed; when sick, the bees do not carry as much more pollen they do when healthy. A sick bee abandons the pollination of flowers earlier than usual and won't be productive in their work as they would have been if healthy.

A sign of sickness in bees is disorientation; a bee when sick becomes disoriented in its movement and activities and tends to get jerky in their acts. Also, the use or the excessive use of chemicals in the hive and the environment can get the bees sick.

Common Pest & Diseases and What to do About Them

The varroa mite is the arch enemy of the bees and their keepers worldwide. The varroa mite is an external parasite and it weakens the bees by attaching itself to them and sucking off their blood; the disease caused by the mite is called the "varroosis". The reproduction of the varroa mite occurs only in the honey bee colony.

Although the varroa mite tops the chart of the threat to bees, there are some other ranges of pests and diseases the honey bee may be affected with. They are:

- ➤ Small hive beetle (Aethina tumida)

- ➤ Leafcutter bee chalkbrood (Ascosphaera aggregata)

- ➤ Tropilaelaps mite (Tropilaelaps clareae)

- ➤ Stonebrood (Aspergillus falvum and Aspergillus fumigatus)

- American foulbrood (Bacillus larvae)

- European foulbrood (Mellissococus pluton)

- Tracheal mite (Acarapis woodi)

- Braula fly (Braula caeca)

The control measures

- The affected hive should be isolated from the rest of the hives.

- Regular and normalized time of inspection.

- Beware of the suppliers where you get your bees from; have a permanent place of supply that are safe and reputable.

- High standards of the dos and don'ts of the apiary should be maintained.

- A perfect standard of hygiene should be maintained in your apiary.

- Sterilize and disinfect your beekeeping equipment time to time.

- Avoid sharing beekeeping equipment and tools with other beekeepers.

- Do not allow room for neglect and commitment issues in the care for your bees.

- Always be on the lookout for pests and diseases

- Stop the use of chemical around your apiary

- Maintain a perfectly hygienic environment for your bees.

Critters You Should Watch Out for

The bees, the honey and the apiary in general tend to attract some animals which are a threat to the apiary and the bees, together with the honey. A preventive measure should be taken against these creatures who come and eat up the bees and the honey they produce. Below are the most common critters to watch out for the moment you create and establish your apiary:

❖ The bear: Naturally, bears are attracted to honey but when the whole apiary is involved, they tend to go bonkers and having discovered one will always go back to it especially if the apiary is left unprotected. They will destroy the equipment and tools used for beekeeping, they will destroy the hive, cause death to many adult bees and do their favorite part of the mission; eat up all the honey. Bears are best prevented by the installation of electric fences. This will manage to keep them at bay and prevent them from paying your apiary a not so friendly visit.

❖ The skunk: The skunks are insectivorous creatures who are addicted to the juice they extract from the bees by chewing them. By their nature for digging up for food, when they discover an apiary, they will dig up all the hives, leaving behind a mess and the destruction of the hives. They are known for spitting out the solid part of the bees after having extracted the juice from their body. If a preventive measure is not procured, the skunks will come back almost, if not every night for your bees. Traps can be used to catch these bee eating creatures.

❖ The hive beetles: they are tiny creatures but a mighty destructive force to the hives; to beekeeping itself. The hive beetles are unwanted guests who are in the habit of making themselves at home inside the hive and start laying eggs immediately, not to talk of them eating up all the bee broods and defecting the honey. These tiny destructive forces increase the stress levels of the bees. Periodic inspection of the hive is highly advised. When you neglect your hive and the hive beetles get their nasty self on your hives, it might lead to the loss of your bees from their hives. Employ proper beekeeping management measures and play your role as a responsible beekeeper.

Maintaining General Hygiene

Overall, the high hygiene maintenance in all aspects of beekeeping is strongly advised. Maintain your own personal hygiene and that of your apiary and your bees. Maintaining good hygiene goes a long way in the help of preventing loss and damage to the keeping of bees. As beekeeper, to maintain good hygiene, you have to:

i. Clean your beekeeping equipment and tools regularly: do not use strong or excessive use of chemicals to disinfect and clean your equipment.

ii. Take very good care of the protective gears you wear: have a special place for them; not in your home and not in your apiary, wash and disinfect them regularly, it protects you and your bees from possible diseases.

iii. Waste materials should not be left lying around the apiary: dispose of them immediately.

iv. Do not leave the job of cleaning up the mold up frames to your bees, it is your responsibility as their keeper.

v. All that can attract and harbor pests are advised to be cleared off; old combs, dead-out colonies and beeswax scraps. Clear them all off regularly.

vi. Be the neatest beekeeper there is; and the best.

You have come to the end of your journey in wanting to learn about the bees, how they work and how they are kept. Hopefully, you will be the best beekeeper there is for these wonderful creatures you now want to take under your wings. Cheers to a fantastic beekeeping journey! And all the best in your new beekeeping journey!

Printed in Great Britain
by Amazon

33296510R00067